The Non-Guide
to the No-Thing

VOLUME THREE

A Simple, Clear Explanation of
What the 'Paradigm Shift' Actually Means

TERRY FAVOUR

AMADO PRESS

AMADO, ARIZONA

The Non-Guide to the No-Thing

VOLUME THREE

TERRY FAVOUR

Library of Congress Control Number: 2010924131

ISBN: 978-0-964-0898-5-3

Amado Press
PO Box 6335
Amado, AZ 85645
Telephone: 800-531-5956
E-mail: info@AmadoPress.com
Website: www.AmadoPress.com

Original illustrations by: Terry Favour
Cover and Interior Design: James Bennett Design

To Bailey, and all
future dedicated thinkers

Introduction

With every day that passes, the self-imposed peril that threatens our planet and our humanity becomes more apparent. We have come a long way over the ages. We have at our fingertips all the information that we need to evolve, once more, into the potential that awaits us. One way or another, undoubtedly, the creativity that makes up our cosmos will take the next step. What I don't know is whether our human forms will take this step willingly, or even successfully. Like spoiled children, we may only step forward after causing ourselves and our planet much pain.

I am just an ordinary person. I am not a scholar, not a spiritual teacher, not a scientist. There is available right now a lot of information provided by qualified people. Armed only with an open mind, the average person can educate himself. We all can become aware of the magnificent discoveries that point the way through this dangerous labyrinth.

It seems that this job has been left up to each one of us, individually. There is no one person or teaching available to save us. Perhaps the maturity necessary to find our own way is embedded in the transition itself. In any case, it has been my good fortune to come across the heartfelt written words of caring scholars, spiritual teachers and scientists. These people are humble folks, reaching out to us, trying to impart the wisdom that their in-depth studies revealed to them. Over the years, their thoughts have become the fabric out of which my own understanding is woven. It is a weave in which I can no longer find the individual threads. I cannot list all these wonderful sources.

This silent tapestry, made from all that wealth of wisdom, whispered to me as I moved around my daily life. Eventually it expressed itself in these little volumes. It is my hope that, in some small way, they can contribute to the monumental effort it will take to free ourselves from the bondage of this worn out paradigm, and propel us safely towards our destiny.

Terry Favour

Here in Black
and White

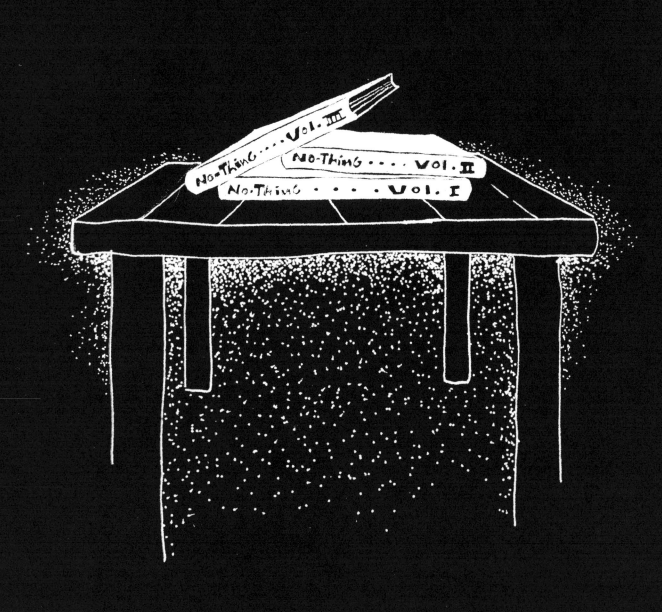

So here we have it: the last of three little books, all black and white.

The very fact that we can read
those words depends on contrast of some kind.
We've all heard someone say, or even said ourselves,
"there it was in black and white."

Our very existence depends on this
contrast, this dualism.

Dualism was covered to a great extent
in Volume 1. Then in Volume 2, I wrote about
how our senses and our minds shape
our perceived reality.

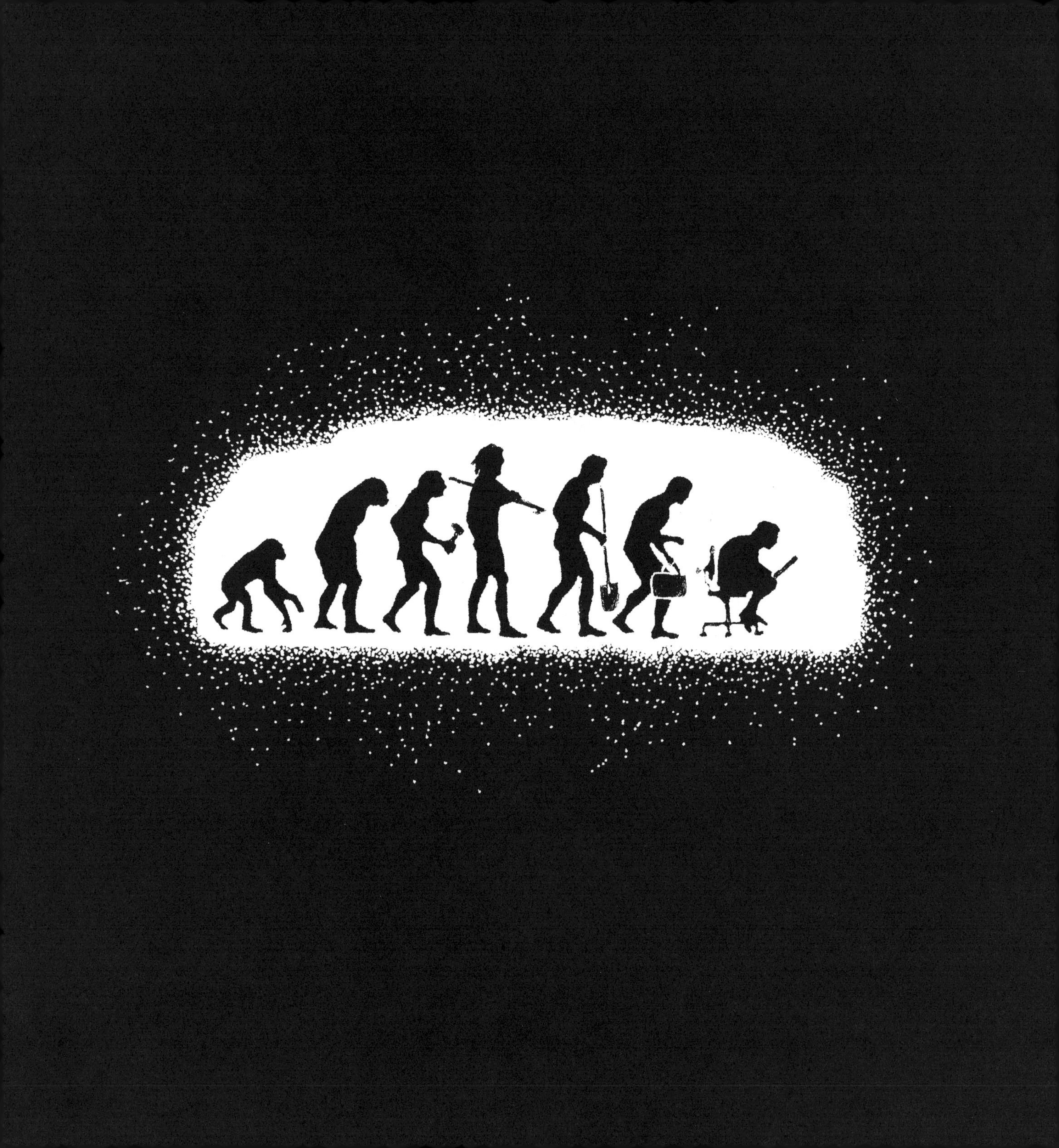

Let us go a little further to better understand how critical this information is to our humanity and to our evolution as a species. It may even affect our continued existence as Homo sapiens on this planet. And, interestingly, it also affects our comfort level, our happiness and our peace.

First, recall, as discussed in Volume 1, that the measurable degrees or attributes of hot and cold, and the concept of temperature, are inseparable. If we have hot and cold—measurable attributes or degrees, then we also have the concept of temperature. If we have the concept of temperature, then we must also have measurable attributes.

LL

the countless pairs of opposites or
contrasting elements that make up our lives
are in this way the same. All combine
measurable attributes with concepts.

Plus

in every case, the concept that accompanies
dualistic pairs, organizes and arranges their 'parts' into a
useful and understandable whole. In the case of temperature
the parts are degrees. From now on, to emphasize this
characteristic, think of it as an 'organizing concept.'

INTELLIGENCE + PRINCIPLE

This organizing concept, by very definition, implies intelligence of some kind, and because it applies to ALL dualistic phenomena, it qualifies as an observable Principle.

Turning again to the example of temperature covered in Volume 2, let's examine for a moment the very important, but often misunderstood and misused, role of perception.

Have you ever found yourself waiting
for a bus or standing in line for a movie, arguing
with a friend about the temperature?

"It's freezing," you say, hugging yourself
to keep warm. "No, it isn't," replies your friend. "It's
very pleasant. Here, take my coat. I'm getting hot."
"But you will be cold," you argue. "No, I won't,"
says your friend, draping her jacket
over your shoulders.

It is not difficult to see that this argument is simply a matter of perception. Maybe you are just getting used to living in Phoenix in the summer. Or maybe your metabolism rate is slower than your friend's.

But you and your friend COULD get caught in a senseless argument, mixing up fact and perception. It happens all the time.

"It is 70 degrees today. I heard it
on the news. The fact is that 70 degrees
is warm," your friend states. "I don't care
about your facts," you respond, "that breeze,
coming from somewhere, is freezing.""Hey,"
your friend says, "I don't feel a breeze.
And 70 degrees is 70 degrees."

As human beings we often assume that
our personal perceptions are fact. Our political and
religious perceptions are obvious cases, and there are subtle
ones as well—our personal views of morality or truth,
for example. While 70 degrees may be a reportable
fact, whether we perceive it as hot or cold is
based on our perception.

That said; let's move back to the discussion of temperature as organizing concept and degrees as measurable attributes.

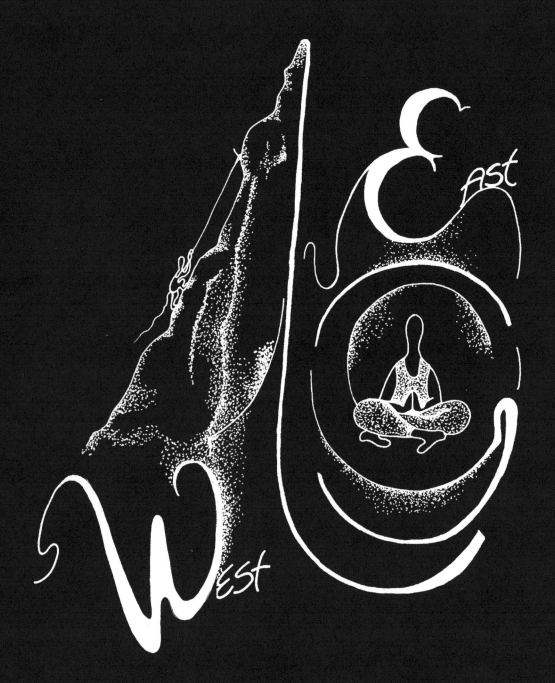

Volumes 1 and 2 referred to the difference between Eastern and Western philosophies.

The Eastern philosophies often speak of form and emptiness. They tell us that the 'ground of all being' is both form and emptiness, and that they are the same thing.

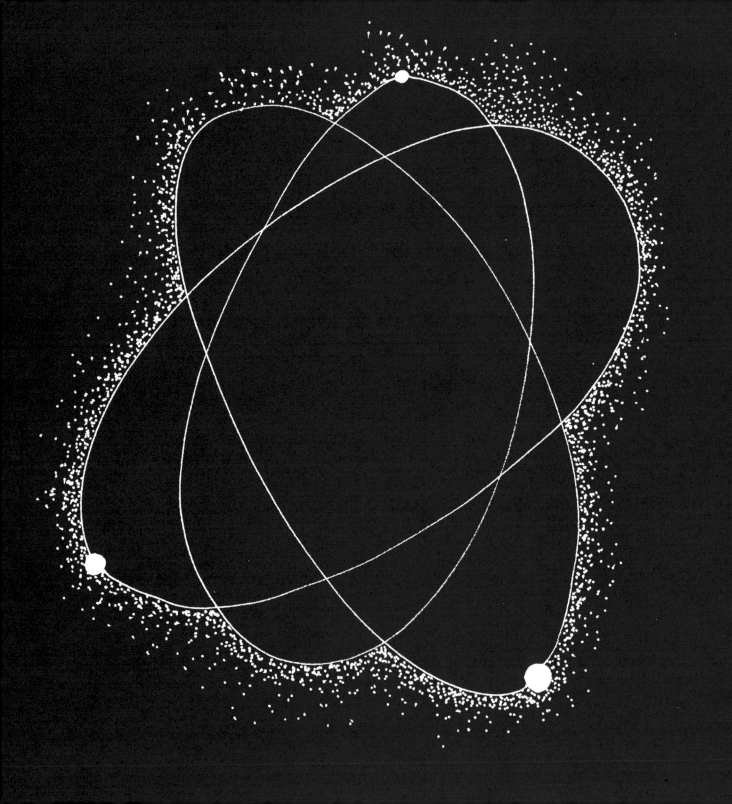

Our relatively recent Western science tells us that objects are not solid, but are composed mostly of vast empty space.

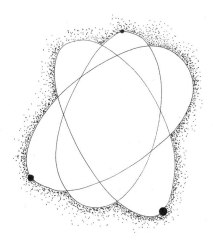

In simplified terms, quantum physics says that waves, which are potential, remain potential until observed, at which time they become particles, which are actual.

It seems that Eastern philosophy and Western science have met.

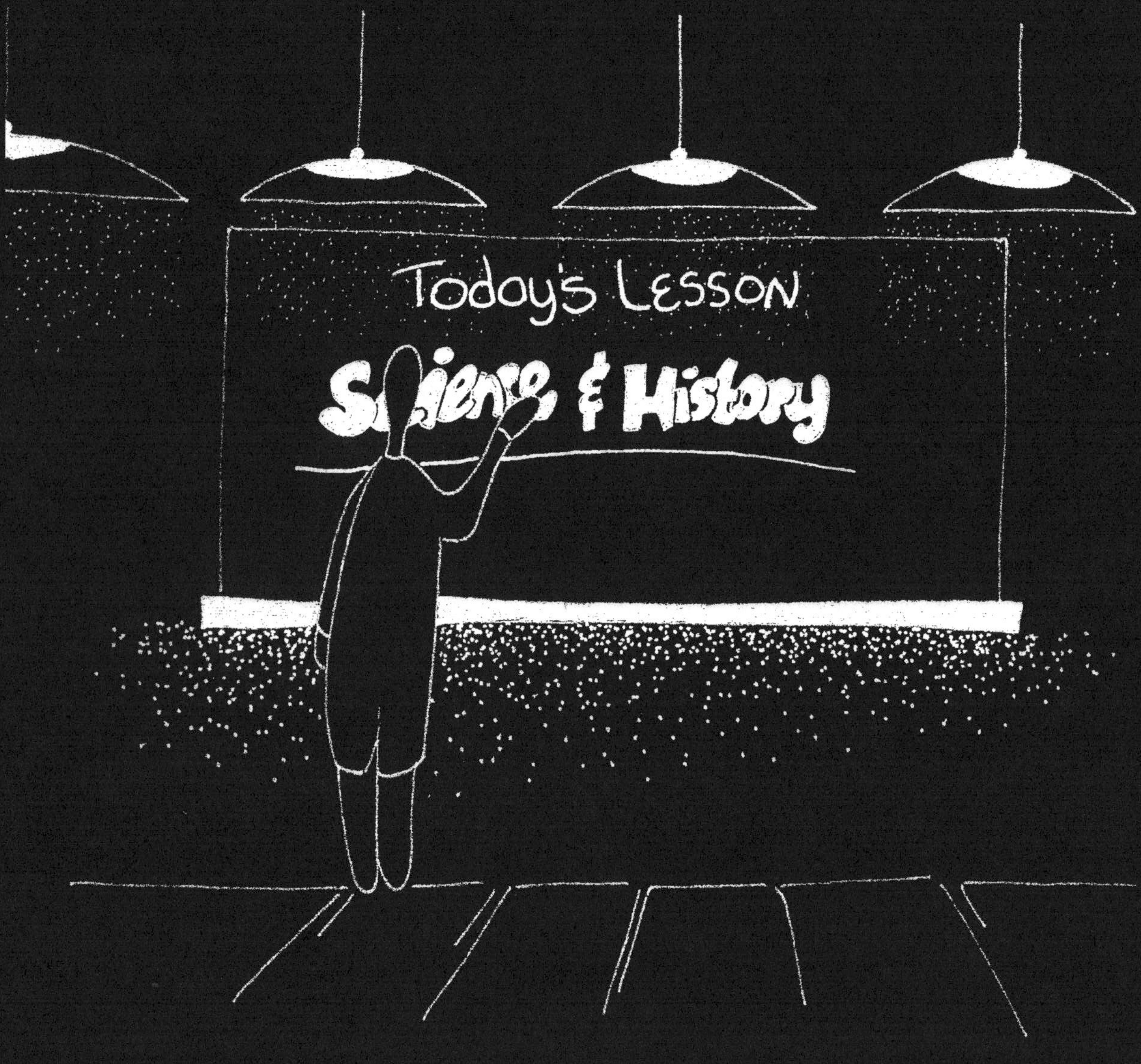
Today's Lesson
& History

Volumes 1 and 2 went into great detail concerning the 'mechanics' behind this interesting reality. I emphasized not only how pairs of opposites act as a conduit that enables consciousness to be, but also how the limiting aspect of our dualistic sense perceptions acts as a separating agent. Our dualistic sense perceptions allow for infinite individual experiences, as well as for the many different collective paradigms that fill our history.

And even though we may understand all
this on an intellectual level, it won't do us much
good until our understanding is experiential—
and can take its rightful place as
our PRESENT paradigm.

That is the whole point. The entire reason
for these little books is to help us all understand
this looming shift, and to open the way
for us to actually experience it.

Most interesting is that although we haven't experienced it, the shift has already occurred. Much of the technology that we use mindlessly every day would not exist without the discoveries of quantum physics.

If we stopped to take a look, we would see that much of our daily discomfort, the time crunch we all experience, for example, is due to the fact that we have one foot in a belief system we do understand, and one foot in a system we don't understand. Without knowing it, we straddle the beliefs and attitudes of Newtonian physics and quantum physics. We mix them, thinking of ourselves in Newtonian terms as solid and separate, while operating in the quantum world of computers, cell phones and virtual reality. Blending these two realities has changed our daily lives as much as or more than anything has ever changed human lives in recorded history.

And to make matters worse, a good portion of the world that makes up our science and should be leading us toward a whole new understanding, does not itself understand the significance of its own discoveries.

WHY?

Because, many years ago, as we approached the era of the scientific revolution—resulting in Newtonian world accomplishments, we absolutely stopped asking the question, "Who are we?" The great minds of that era, assumed that that question was unanswerable scientifically, and thought it would get in the way of objective scientific research. They thought such a question should be left to the more subjective, philosophical or religious thinkers. Our quest became, instead, to expand our own power and to 'make nature do our bidding.'

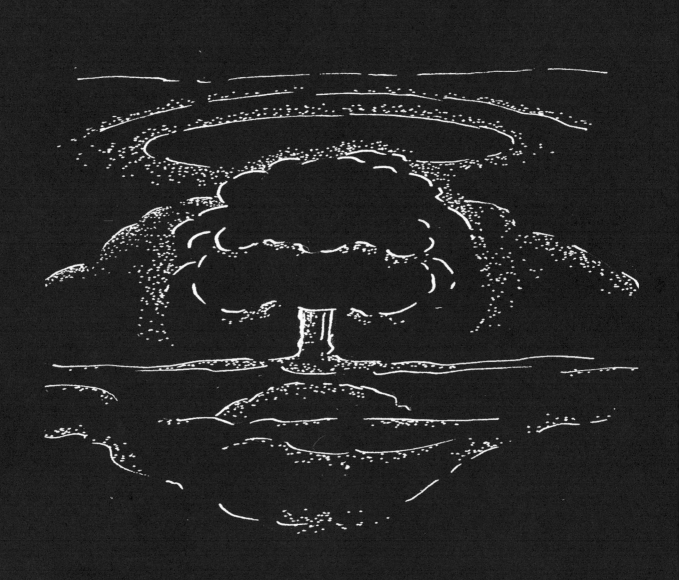

If you don't ask the right question, you won't get the right answer. Now the times have changed and the modern scientific community's failure to ask the question, "Who are we?" has lethal potential.

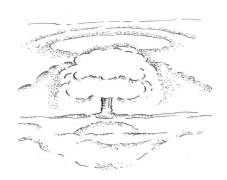

This out-of-date, blatant omission
of the vital question that even the youngest
of us has sense enough to ask, has placed us
on the brink of our own destruction.

Let us all ask it now.

WHO ARE WE?

Who are we? And how will the analogy of temperature, picked out of the infinite number of pairs of opposites, help us?

How will that duo of 'concept and measurable attributes' that we deemed an 'observable Principle' help us know who we are?

It helps us because that 'duo' is a 'Principle'
and that Principle applies to all pairs of opposites,
all contrasting elements, everything dualistic.

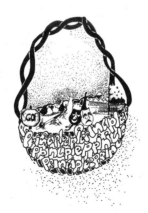

UT

this duo is the Big One:

IT APPLIES TO FORM AND EMPTINESS

The East has always talked about form and emptiness. The West now finds it an intricate part of its science (waves and particles). Both systems of thought would have to concur that form and emptiness are the 'ground of all being.'

Our use of temperature is an example of
the observable Principle. Is not temperature also
an example of form and emptiness? The organizational
concept of temperature is not measurable, is not a
thing, and is therefore empty. Degrees of temperature
are measurable, and therefore have form.

MEASURABLE AND IMMEASURABLE ARE ALSO 'FORM AND EMPTINESS'

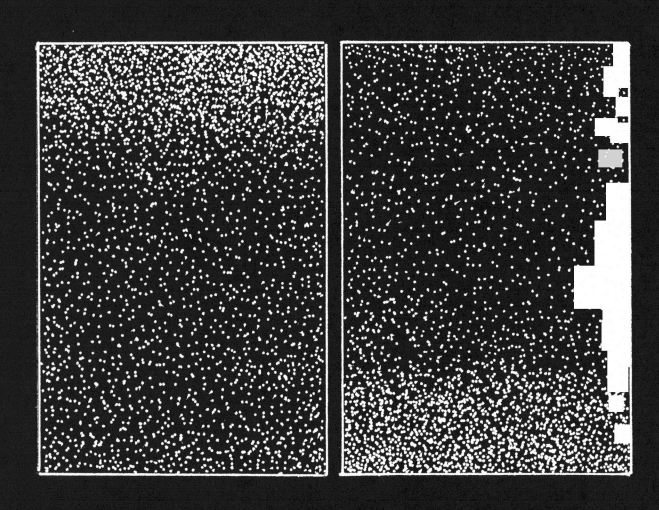

Besides all this, quantum physics has shown us that FORM is not so solid, and EMPTINESS is not so empty.

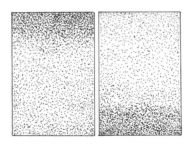

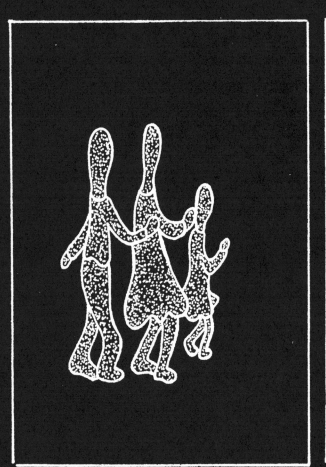

And since our world is dualistic,
we live and move around in an environment
made up entirely of

EMPTINESS AND FORM

To reiterate, all the contrasting elements of this world that are measurable are objects, which also have immeasurable organizing concepts. The measurable and the immeasurable are inseparable. The Principle that is the 'ground of all being' is that 'form and emptiness— measurable and immeasurable' are two aspects of the same thing.

That Principle applies to us too. Each of us is, individually, both a measurable body living in time and space, and also an immeasurable organizing concept. This organizing concept is clearly known to us. IT IS INTELLIGENCE! The very definition of an organizing concept implies intelligence of some kind.

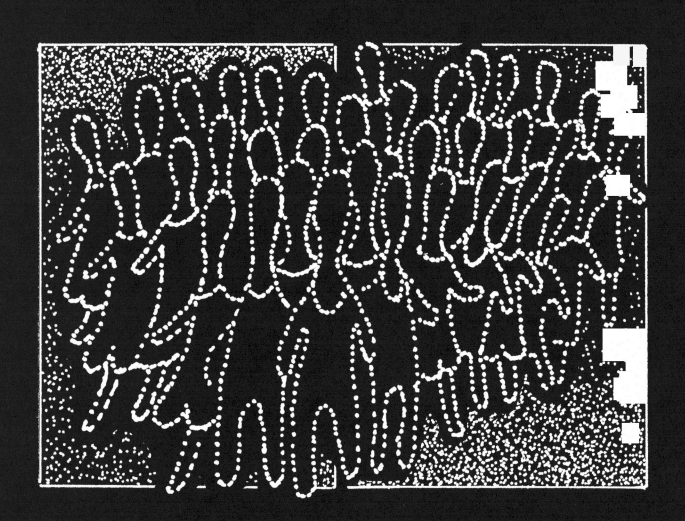

That Principle also applies to us collectively as a human race, as well as to everything known to us.

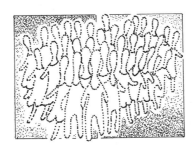

Over and over in these volumes, I have
shown examples that even measurable objects
are not made of material stuff. I have shown that
measurable and immeasurable are actually
two different aspects of the same thing.

Whether it is a seed we planted, growing in our garden, or a rock we use as a paperweight, or even a plastic water bottle we take on a hike, all these objects are products of and dependent on an organizing concept. That organizing concept has as its basis intelligence, and is this Principle.

LET US NOW ASK SOME VERY POINTED QUESTIONS.

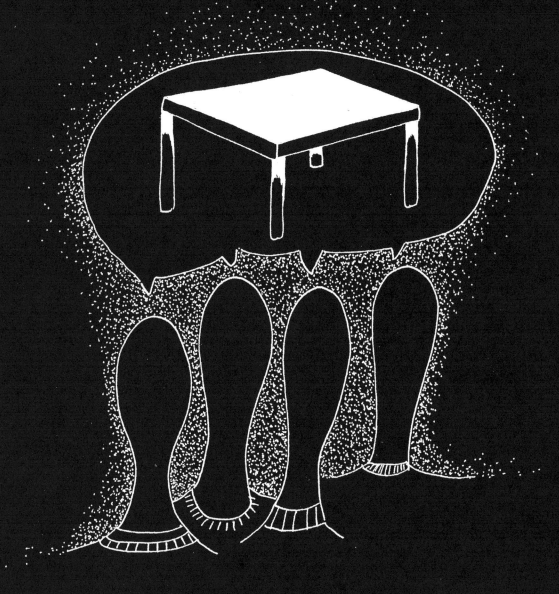

In order for this intelligence to manifest into things, must it not have a focus of attention? Do not our sense perceptions and our minds, as described in Volume 2, provide that focus? Is this not the same focus of attention that the scientist uses to observe that wave that becomes a particle? And are his instruments not an extension of his senses?

When this scientist and his instruments focus
on that wave, is the scientist himself not an example
of our collective human potential? Does the very fact
that he has a body with a unique set of sense perceptions,
not make it impossible for him to be an independent observer?
Like the argument debating whether 70 degrees is hot or cold,
is the scientist not limited by the 'tool' that is his body?
Furthermore, is he not using a mind that is part of a
collective paradigm, based on his fraternity of fellow
scientists, his religious affiliation, on and on—until
his personal views combine with the
present collective paradigm?

Are we caught in a squirrel cage? Are we running around and around in a system of our own making, only to break out of it every few centuries to create a new, but just as confining, cage to run around in—AGAIN?

So let's stop. Let's take a breath.
Let's slow down enough to ask
the right question.

WHO ARE WE?

Coupled with the wealth of current
and timeless information, can we be very
very still? Can we silently ask the question,
"Who are we?"

With all that we know now, can we
listen for that intelligence, that organizing
Principle, that we know that we are?

Can we be still enough to realize that when ALL else is silent, what is left is the 'ground of our own being,' and of all beings from which ALL becomes manifest?

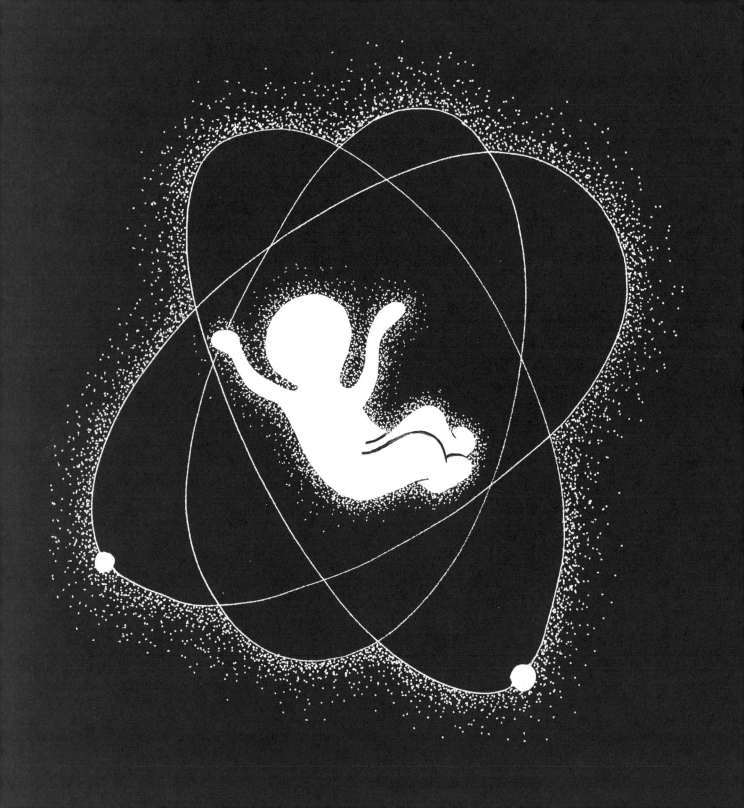

And from the silent depths of our beings, can
we feel what the next action should be? Can we tap
into our own supremely intelligent, organizing Principle—
the same Principle of intelligence smart enough to grow a
baby, smart enough to create the entire solar system? Are
we mature enough to get over our own importance and
step into the truth of our beings—that are not separate
from, but are an integral part of the whole system?
Are we ready to stop suffering?

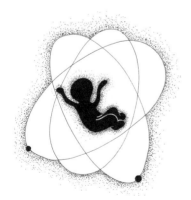

In truth, our time is up. Our childhood
is over. If we can't make this simple leap that
requires absolutely no faith at all—due to our
quantum discoveries, then we are truly
expendable and unworthy.
HOWEVER

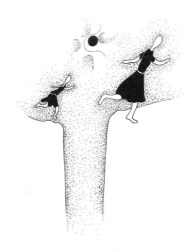

One way or another, thanks to the organizing Principle itself, this ever-expanding evolving consciousness that we are will continue expanding … growing …

For …
EXPANSION IS ITS VERY NATURE!

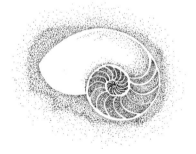

117

ACKNOWLEDGMENTS

As I wrote and illustrated these little books, I had no idea that I would publish them. I had no idea how to publish them. When Alexandra Shamaya, my publisher, encouraged me to consider this possibility, it was the energy that accompanied her invitation that sealed the deal. Without Alexandra this could not have happened. She put me together with James Bennett, a book designer of extraordinary talent, who infused professionalism into my work. Nearly at the same time, a serendipitous coincidence introduced me to Karen Meadows, my editor. Karen unobtrusively sat with me and shaped my words in such a seamless way that I can hardly detect the changes. To you three I wish to acknowledge this indebtedness ... and extend my undying gratitude.

Terry with her grand daughter

When the author, Terry Favour, first asked the question "Who Are We?" her very ability to form such thoughts and sentences was just beginning. The failure of those around her to answer back, set her on a quest that would last indefinitely. The process led her across a diversified terrain, weaving back and forth through spiritual philosophy and science, from East to West.

As an adult she has sustained herself and this passion working as an artist and designer, owning and operating a small ethnic arts company with her son, located in Northern New Mexico. In the 1980s she became interested in the Enneagram. In 2004 she and her daughter studied under David Daniels and Helen Palmer and they both became certified Enneagram teachers.

She feels that expanding one's limitations should be an unending endeavor so she continues this life work every day. It was her grown children who led her to write these three little books, stating that she had a knack for simplifying complicated matters.

She continues to draw and write and she lives in Santa Fe NM with her husband and her cat.